Should the United States Have OPEN BORDERS?

By Amy Holt

KidHaven Publishing

Published in 2021 by
KidHaven Publishing, an Imprint of Greenhaven Publishing, LLC
353 3rd Avenue
Suite 255
New York, NY 10010

Designer: Deanna Paternostro
Editor: Jennifer Lombardo

Photo credits: Cover Chad Zuber/Shutterstock.com; p. 5 (main) Christopher Furlong/Getty Images; p. 5 (inset) JNEZAM/Shutterstock.com; p. 7 (top) Katherine Welles/Shutterstock.com; p. 7 (bottom) Bill Pugliano/Getty Images; p. 9 Ebtikar/Shutterstock.com; p. 11 (main) Jan Sochor/Latincontent/Getty Images; p. 11 (inset) AJR_photo/Shutterstock.com; p. 13 Mario Tama/Getty Images; p. 15 (main) North Wind Picture Archives/Alamy Stock Photo; p. 15 (inset) Jonathan Wiggs/The Boston Globe via Getty Images; p. 17 (top) Bettmann/Bettmann/Getty Images; p. 17 (bottom) Michael Maslan/Corbis/VCG via Getty Images; p. 17 (inset) The Food Group/Shutterstock.com; p. 19 Monkey Business Images/Shutterstock.com; p. 21 (notepad) ESB Professional/Shutterstock.com; p. 21 (markers) Kucher Serhii/Shutterstock.com; p. 21 (photo frame) FARBAI/iStock/Thinkstock; p. 21 (inset, left) David A. Litman/Shutterstock.com; p. 21 (inset, middle) Jeffrey Greenberg/Universal Images Group via Getty Images; p. 21 (inset, right) Jacob Lund/Shutterstock.com.

Library of Congress Cataloging-in-Publication Data

Names: Holt, Amy, author.
Title: Should the United States have open borders? / Amy Holt.
Description: First edition. | New York : KidHaven Publishing, 2021. | Series: Points of view | Includes index.
Identifiers: LCCN 2019050608 (print) | LCCN 2019050609 (ebook) | ISBN 9781534534308 (library binding) | ISBN 9781534534285 (paperback) | ISBN 9781534534315 (ebook) | ISBN 9781534534292 (set)
Subjects: LCSH: Emigration and immigration–Juvenile literature. | Border patrols–United States–Juvenile literature. | United States–Emigration and immigration–Juvenile literature.
Classification: LCC JV6035 .H65 2021 (print) | LCC JV6035 (ebook) | DDC 325.73–dc23
LC record available at https://lccn.loc.gov/2019050608
LC ebook record available at https://lccn.loc.gov/2019050609

Printed in the United States of America

Some of the images in this book illustrate individuals who are models. The depictions do not imply actual situations or events.

CPSIA compliance information: Batch #BS20K: For further information contact Greenhaven Publishing LLC, New York, New York at 1-844-317-7404.

Please visit our website, www.greenhavenpublishing.com. For a free color catalog of all our high-quality books, call toll free 1-844-317-7404 or fax 1-844-317-7405.

CONTENTS

Borders and Immigration 4

Open or Closed? 6

Helping Other People 8

Worried About Safety 10

Nothing to Fear 12

Worries About Jobs 14

Making the Country Better 16

Losing Meaning 18

Looking at Both Sides 20

Glossary 22

For More Information 23

Index 24

Borders and IMMIGRATION

A border is a line that separates one country from another. You can see the borders drawn on maps, but you often can't see them in real life. However, many people in the United States have very strong feelings about their country's borders—and about who's allowed to cross them.

Someone who leaves one country to live in another is called an immigrant. Arguments about borders are often connected to arguments about how easy or hard it is for people to immigrate to the United States. It's important to know all the facts before forming an opinion about these issues.

Know the Facts!

When anyone is allowed to cross a border any time, that's called an open border. When people or goods can't cross a border, that border is closed. Most countries don't have completely open or completely closed borders.

The border between Germany and France (below) is open; anyone can cross at any time. The border between North and South Korea (left) is closed; most people are never allowed to cross.

Open or CLOSED?

Most borders aren't completely closed. Instead, they're regulated, which means someone checks to make sure people have permission to cross. Some borders are **stricter** than others, and some people think the United States should have strict border rules. Others think U.S. borders should be more open.

People have different ideas about what having "open borders" means. Most people who support open borders for the United States generally think it should be easier to get into the country, but they still think there should be some rules. Other people think the borders of the country should be completely open, like they are between states.

Know the Facts!

Common reasons people immigrate to the United States include already having a family member in the country, being offered a job, or seeking **asylum**.

A person who wants to enter the United States has to show their **passport** at the border to prove they're allowed to enter. Once they're in the country, though, they can move freely between states.

Helping Other PEOPLE

One reason why some people think open borders are a good thing is that it makes it easier for immigrants to come into a new country. Often, these immigrants are running away from **violence** or **poverty** in their old country. Some countries make it easy for them to get permission from the government to live there.

The U.S. immigration rules are so strict that it can take months or years for someone to get permission to immigrate. Many immigrants say getting this permission is confusing, hard, and expensive. Sometimes people are refused entry even if they do everything right. Most people don't want completely open borders, but they do want the immigration process to be improved, or made better.

Know the Facts!

In 2019, it was announced that the United States planned to let 18,000 **refugees** into the country in 2020.

To many people, "open borders" means making the immigration process easier for people who want to come to the United States to live.

Worried About SAFETY

People who oppose open borders are often nervous about who might be coming into the United States. They worry that the same people who are making it unsafe to live in other parts of the world could come to the United States and make life there less safe too. Some Americans are also worried about open borders leading to more acts of **terrorism**.

People who feel this way think the United States should make it very hard for people to come into the country. They say it's important to keep the people who already live there safe by keeping the borders closed to people who can't be trusted.

Know the Facts!

Studies have shown that most terrorist attacks in the United States are done by people who were born there, but many Americans still worry about immigrants from countries that deal with a lot of terrorism.

Some Americans worry that open borders will make it easier for people who cause harm, such as gang members and terrorists, to come to the United States. Most people who want to immigrate to the United States don't want to cause harm, but many people think it's still a good idea to check who's coming into the country.

Nothing to FEAR

People who support more open borders point to studies that show that immigrants are less likely to **commit** crimes than people who were born in the country. In fact, many immigrants come to the United States to get away from crime in their home country. Imagine if your neighborhood was very unsafe, but you weren't allowed to move!

People don't generally move to a new country unless they have a good reason. If that reason is safety, people are going to leave no matter what. If they're refused entry at the border, they have nowhere safe to go.

Know the Facts!

The United Nations (UN) says freedom of movement is a human right. Some people say borders should be more open so it's easier for people to move if they want to.

Crossing the border is very unsafe for people who need to leave their country but can't get into the United States legally. For example, many people get sick or hurt in the desert when they try to immigrate from Mexico. Having open borders would make it safer for people to immigrate.

Worries About JOBS

Many people who support strict border laws worry that if there are too many immigrants in the United States, there won't be enough jobs for everyone. Some of them worry that immigrants will take all the jobs. Others think that immigrants won't get jobs at all and will just live off of **welfare programs** that are paid for with workers' taxes.

People who don't support open borders generally like the fact that someone who wants to immigrate to the United States often needs to prove they have a certain skill they can use to help the country. They think too many unskilled immigrants will be bad for the U.S. **economy**.

Know the Facts!

As of 2018, 17 percent of workers in the United States were immigrants. Immigrants were less likely to be unemployed than people who were born in the United States.

For years, people have worried that new immigrants will take all the jobs and leave none for the people who were born in the United States. This is part of the reason why some people don't like to hire immigrants.

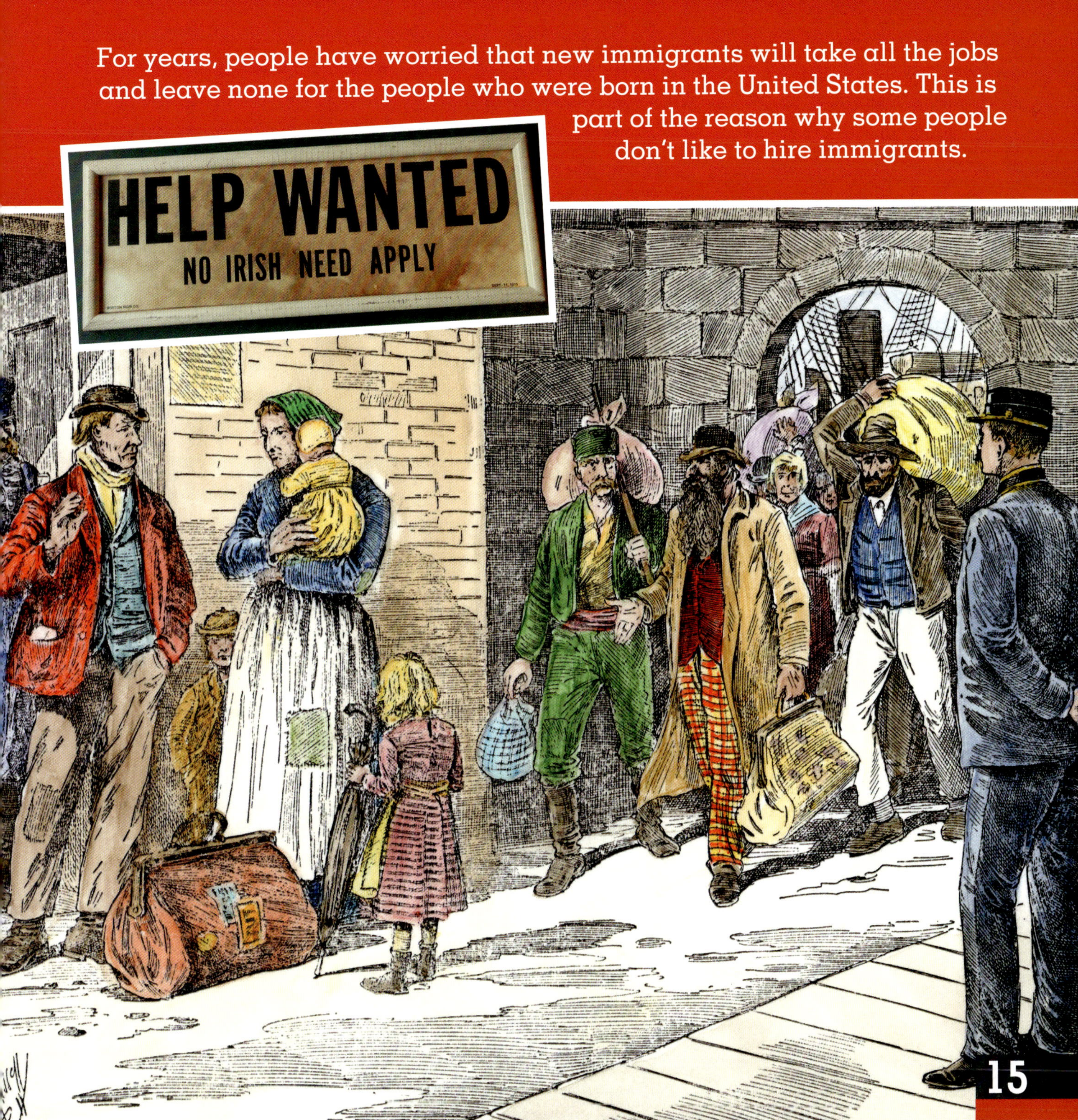

Making the Country

BETTER

People who support open borders point to studies that show that immigrants make a country's economy better. Immigrants don't often look for the same jobs as people born in the United States. Because of this, they don't take jobs away from people who are already in the country. Immigrants also introduce people to new ideas, foods, and activities.

Many people say that in the past, having more open borders was a big part of what made the United States a great country. They think it's important to keep letting people in because everyone has something they can do for the country.

Know the Facts!

Except for Native Americans, everyone who lives in the United States today is here because they or their **ancestors** were immigrants. This is why American **culture** is mostly made up of parts of other cultures.

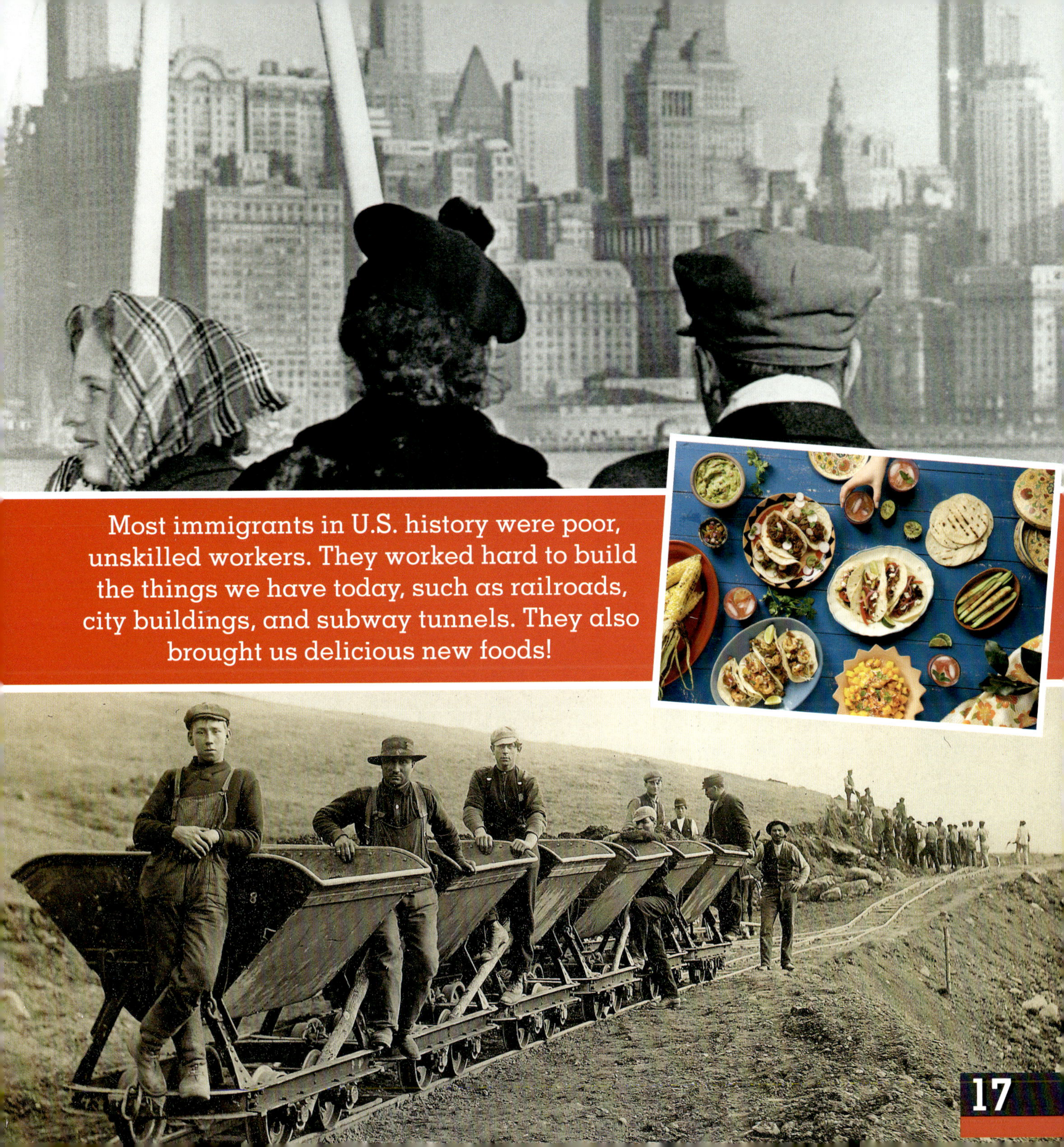

Most immigrants in U.S. history were poor, unskilled workers. They worked hard to build the things we have today, such as railroads, city buildings, and subway tunnels. They also brought us delicious new foods!

Losing MEANING

Many people who oppose open borders don't think everyone should be welcome in a country. They think the United States should only let in people who care a lot about being American. Some people say that if borders stop mattering, people won't have pride in their country anymore. Without pride, they say, no one will want to make the country better. They'll just leave when they get tired of it.

Some people also worry that if the United States has open borders, being American won't mean anything anymore. If it isn't hard to move to a new country, they say, why would nationality matter? They worry that if nationality loses meaning, their **identity** as Americans will also lose its meaning.

Know the Facts!

In 2018, 47 percent of Americans said they were very proud of their nationality.

Many people who live in the United States, including people who were born in another country, are proud to be Americans. Some worry that open borders would take away this part of who they are.

Looking at

BOTH SIDES

There are many arguments for and against open borders. People who oppose them worry mostly about safety and the economy. People who support them often want to make life better for the people who are trying to move to the United States. Many people don't want the borders to be either completely open or closed. Some want the laws to be stricter, while others want the laws to be less strict.

Now that you know the arguments, think about both sides. Do you think the United States should have open borders? How strict do you think U.S. border laws should be?

Know the Facts!

While he was running for president, Donald Trump promised to build a wall on the U.S.–Mexico border to make it harder for people to immigrate without permission. What do you think of this idea?

Should the United States have open borders?

YES

- It would make it easier for people to leave a country where they're unsafe or poor.
- Immigrants help a country's economy.
- Americans and immigrants often don't look for the same jobs.
- The United States became the place it is today because of immigrants who wanted to help their new country.

NO

- It might make it easier for people who cause harm to come to the United States.
- Letting in a lot of people who don't have special skills might make the economy worse.
- If there are too many immigrants, it might be hard for Americans to find jobs.
- If we don't have borders, Americans might lose their identity.

There are many arguments for and against having strict border laws. What do you think about these arguments?

GLOSSARY

ancestors: People in your family who lived long before you.

asylum: The protection given by a country to someone who has left their home country because they were afraid for their safety.

commit: To do something that is often illegal or harmful.

culture: The beliefs and ways of life of a certain group of people.

economy: The way in which goods and services are made, sold, and used in a country or area.

identity: The way someone feels about themselves.

passport: An official document issued by the government of a country that identifies someone as a citizen of that country and that is generally necessary when crossing a regulated border.

poverty: The state of being poor.

refugee: A person who is escaping war, a natural disaster, or some other problem in their home country.

strict: Strongly enforcing rules and discipline.

terrorism: The use of violent acts to scare people as a way of trying to achieve a goal.

violence: The use of physical force to damage or hurt something or someone.

welfare program: A plan of action for poor or unemployed people that helps pay for their food, housing, and other important costs.

For More
INFORMATION

WEBSITES

Scholastic: "Immigration: Stories of Yesterday and Today"
teacher.scholastic.com/activities/immigration/index.htm
Learn more about real immigrant kids, see how immigration has changed over the years, and take a virtual tour of Ellis Island, which used to be the first stop for new immigrants to the United States.

***TIME for Kids*: "Border Fight"**
www.timeforkids.com/g34/border-fight
This article explains some of the reasons why people disagree about whether U.S. borders should be open or closed.

BOOKS

Caplan, Bryan Douglas, Zach Weinersmith, and Mary Cagle. *Open Borders: The Science and Ethics of Immigration*. New York, NY: First Second, 2019.

Osborne, Linda Barnett. *This Land Is Our Land: A History of American Immigration*. New York, NY: Abrams, 2016.

Otfinoski, Steven. *Immigration & America*. New York, NY: Scholastic, 2018.

Publisher's note to educators and parents: Our editors have carefully reviewed these websites to ensure that they are suitable for students. Many websites change frequently, however, and we cannot guarantee that a site's future contents will continue to meet our high standards of quality and educational value. Be advised that students should be closely supervised whenever they access the Internet.

INDEX

A

asylum, 6

C

closed borders, 4, 5, 10, 14, 20
crimes, 12
cultures, 16

E

economies, 14, 16, 20, 21

G

gangs, 11

H

human rights, 12

I

immigration, 4, 6, 8, 9, 10, 11, 12, 13, 14, 15, 16, 17, 20, 21

J

jobs, 6, 14, 15, 16, 21

M

Mexico, 13, 20

N

Native Americans, 16

P

poverty, 8

R

refugees, 8

S

safety, 10, 12, 20

T

terrorism, 10, 11
Trump, Donald, 20

U

United Nations (UN), 12

V

violence, 8

W

welfare, 14